• HBJ READING PROGRAM •

RIBBONS

 LAUREATE EDITION

LEVEL 4

Bernice E. Cullinan
Roger C. Farr
W. Dorsey Hammond
Nancy L. Roser
Dorothy S. Strickland

HBJ **HARCOURT BRACE JOVANOVICH, PUBLISHERS**
Orlando   San Diego   Chicago   Dallas

Acknowledgments

For permission to reprint copyrighted material, grateful acknowledgment is made to the following sources:

Adam and Charles Black Publishers and Clarkson N. Potter, Inc.: Adapted from *Two Hoots and the King* by Helen Cresswell. Text copyrighted © 1977 by Helen Cresswell. Originally published in the United Kingdom by Ernest Benn Ltd.

Edith Battles: From *Eddie Couldn't Find the Elephants* by Edith Battles. Text © 1974 by Edith Battles.

Grosset & Dunlap, Inc.: Adapted from *Mr. Pine's Storybook* (Titled: "Mr. Pine's Town") by Leonard Kessler. Copyright © 1982 by Leonard Kessler.

Harper & Row Publisher, Inc.: Text and illustrations from "Clouds" in *Mouse Tales,* written and illustrated by Arnold Lobel. Copyright © 1962 by Arnold Lobel. "A Wish Is Quite a Tiny Thing" from *FOR DAYS AND DAYS: A Year-Round Treasury of Child Verse* by Annette Wynne. Copyright 1919 by Harper & Row Publishers, Inc., renewed 1947 by Annette Wynne. Published by J.B. Lippincott.

Highlights for Children, Inc., Columbus, OH: "The Yellow Monster" by Joanna Cargill from *Highlights for Children,* February 1967. Copyright © 1967 by Highlights for Children, Inc.

Karen S. Solomon: "How Wise is an Owl" by Ilo Orleans from *The Zoo That Grew.* Published by Henry Z. Walck, Inc.

Franklin Watts, Inc.: Adapted from *Come! Sit! Stay!* by Joan M. Lexau. Text copyright © 1984 by Joan M. Lexau.

Key: (l)–Left; (r)–Right; (c)–Center; (t)–Top; (b)–Bottom

Photographs

Page iv, HBJ Photo; v, HBJ Photo/Beverly Brosius; vi, E. Streichan; 12, Henry Deters/Monkmeyer Press Photo Service; 13, 14, HBJ Photo; 15, Tom Grill/Comstock, Inc.; 34(t), NASA from H. Armstrong Roberts, Inc.; 34(cl), Jeffrey Myers/FPG; 34(cr), HBJ Photo; 34(b), H. Armstrong Roberts, Inc., 35, NASA; 66, August Upitis/Shostal Associates; 67(t), Gail Greig/Shostal Associates; 67(b), Frances Bannett/DPI; 68(t), Leonard Lee Rue III; 68(b), Robert Ashworth/Photo Researchers; 69(l), Index Stock International; 69(r), Henry Monroe/DPI; 71, NASA; 72, HBJ Photo/Beverly Brosius; 98-99, Coco McCoy/Rainbow; 100-101, HBJ Photo/John Bateman; 102, HBJ Photo/John Bateman; 103, HBJ Photo/John Bateman; 107, HBJ Photo/Beverly Brosius; 108,109, E. Sreichan/T.P.S.; 122(l), Grant Heilman; 122(r), HBJ Photo; 123(tl), HBJ Photo/Beverly Brosius; 123(bl), HBJ Photo/Beverly Brosius; 123(tr), HBJ Photo/Beverly Brosius; 123(br), HBJ Photo/John Bateman; 124(tl), Paul Conklin/Monkmeyer Press Photo Service; 124(bl), Dan McCoy/Rainbow; 124(tr), Paul Conklin/Monkmeyer Press Photo Service; 124(br), Dan McCoy/Rainbow; 125(tl), Mark Antman/Image Works; 125(bl), HBJ Photo/Beverly Brosius; 125(tr), Mark Antman/Image Works; 125(br), Em Ahart; 126(l), HBJ Photo; 126(r), Tom Meyers; 127(t), Kathruyn Muus; 127(b), Art Attack; 157, E. Streichan/T.P.S.

Illustrators

Lynn Adams: pp. 30-31; Terry Anderson: pp. 76-83; Ellen Appleby: pp. 104-105; Len Ebert: pp. 58-65, 128-129; Ethel Gold: pp. 26-29; Meryl Henderson: pp. 120-121; for reference Leonard Kessler: pp. 130-137; Robert Korta: pp. iii, 2-3, 33; Dora Leder: pp. 6-11; Bruce Lemerise: pp. 4-5, 36-37, 74-75, 110-111; Susan Lexa: pp. 24-25; Arnold Lobel: pp. 148-155; Darcy May: pp. 56-57, 112-119; Mary McLaren: pp. 159-177; Yoshi Miyake: pp. 48-55; Bill Ogden: pp. 138-147; Joyce Orchard: pp. 90-97; Sally Schaedler: pp. 16-23, 84-89; Jerry Smath: pp. 38-47.
Cover: Barbara Lanza

Contents

Unit 1
Rainbows 2

Read on Your Own 4

The Yellow Monster 6
by Joanna Cargill (Realistic Fiction)
from THE YELLOW MONSTER

The Bulldozer 12
by Edward D. Mullett (Informational
Article)

Blue Bikes 16
by Margaret Braden (Realistic Fiction)

Sequence 24
(Comprehension Study)

Paint a Rainbow 26
by Althea Rahz (Informational
Article)

The Rainbow 30
  Anonymous (Poem)

Thinking About "Rainbows" 32

Unit 2
Near and Far 34

Read on Your Own 36

Mr. Fig Finds the Sun! 38
  by Bernard Wiseman (Fantasy)

Antonyms 46
  (Vocabulary Study)

Little Feet and Long Walk 48
  by Florence Thompson (Realistic Fiction)

A Wish Is Quite a Tiny Thing 56
  by Annette Wynne (Poem)

**Eddie Couldn't Find the
Elephants** 58
  by Edith Battles (Realistic Fiction)
  from EDDIE COULDN'T FIND
  THE ELEPHANTS

Animals 66
   by Janet C. Bosma   (Informational
   Article)

**Thinking About
"Near and Far"** 70

Unit 3
Winks and Blinks 72

Read on Your Own 74

Come! Sit! Stay! 76
   by Joan M. Lexau   (Realistic Fiction)
   from COME! SIT! STAY!

The Little Casa 84
   by Carolyn Wills   (Realistic Fiction)

Two Hoots and the King 90
   by Helen Cresswell   (Fantasy)
   from TWO HOOTS AND
   THE KING

How Wise Is an Owl 98
   by Ilo Orleans   (Poem)

What Faces Can Show 100
by Leona H. Biz (Informational
Article)

Follow Directions 104
(Study Skills)

**Thinking About "Winks and
Blinks"** 106

Unit 4
Old Days, Old Ways . . 108

Read on Your Own 110

Grandma's Birthday Surprise 112
by Corrine C. Oldham (Realistic
Fiction)

Relate Pictures to Text 120
(Comprehension Study)

All About Signs 122
by Wanda Fortney
(Informational Article)

The Safety Song 128
by Margaret Lowery   (Song)
from GROWING WITH MUSIC

Mr. Pine's Town 130
story and pictures by Leonard Kessler
(Realistic Fiction) from MR. PINE'S
STORYBOOK

The Boy Who Called Wolf 138
an AESOP'S FABLE   (Play)

Bonus: Clouds 148
story and pictures by Arnold Lobel
(Fantasy) from MOUSE TALES

**Thinking About "Old Days,
Old Ways"** 156

Word Helper 159

Word List 179

Awards

The authors and illustrators of selections in this book have received the following awards either for their work in this book or for another of their works. The specific award is indicated under the medallion on the opening page of each award-winning selection.

American Institute of Graphic Arts Book Show
The American Book Award
Irma Simonton Black Award
Randolph Caldecott Medal
Carnegie Medal
Child Study Children's Book Committee at Bank Street College
   Award
Children's Choices
Christopher Award
New York Times Best Illustrated Children's Books of the Year
John Newbery Honor Award
Charlie May Simon Children's Book Award
George G. Stone Center for Children's Books Recognition
   of Merit Award

Rainbows

Rainbows have many colors.

Red, orange, yellow, green, blue, and purple are the colors of the rainbow.

The stories in "Rainbows" have colors, too.

One story is about something that is big, yellow, and easy to see.

You will read a story about two blue bikes.

As you read the stories, look for some of these colors.

Look to see why colors are important in the stories in "Rainbows."

Read on Your Own

Bicycles Are Fun to Ride *by Dorothy Chlad. Childrens Press.* A boy and his friends have fun with their bikes.

Building a House *by Byron Barton. Greenwillow.* Step by step, watch workers build a house.

Miffy's Bicycle *by Dick Bruna. Price Stern Sloan.* A little rabbit dreams of the fun she will have when she has her own bike.

Machines *by Anne and Harlow Rockwell. Macmillan.* A boy tells about the things in his house, his bike, construction machines, and how they work.

Babar's Book of Color *by Laurent de Brunhoff. Random House.* Babar's children and a nephew mix colors to paint pictures.

The Chick and the Duckling *by Mirra Ginsburg. Macmillan.* Why does a chick want to be the same as a duckling?

Peter Spier's Rain *by Peter Spier. Doubleday.* A brother and sister watch a rainstorm from inside their house.

Rain *by Robert Kalan. Greenwillow.* Can you see colors in rain? When the rain stops, there is a rainbow.

Some boys and girls go to see a big yellow monster.
What is the monster?

The Yellow Monster

by Joanna Cargill

Nina ran to Tim's house.

"Come and see a monster,"
Nina said to Tim.
"It is big and yellow.
It is near my house."

"I don't know if I want
to see a monster," said Tim.

"You don't have to be afraid.
You can just watch the monster.
You don't have to get too near it,"
said Nina.

"I will come with you," said Tim.
"Let's get Rick, too."

Nina and Tim ran to get Rick.
"You must see the monster!
It is a big, yellow, helping monster.
It likes to dig.
Follow us, Rick," said Nina.

"I will follow you.
Let's get Linda, too," said Rick.
"She likes to watch monsters."

So Nina, Tim, and Rick ran
to get Linda.

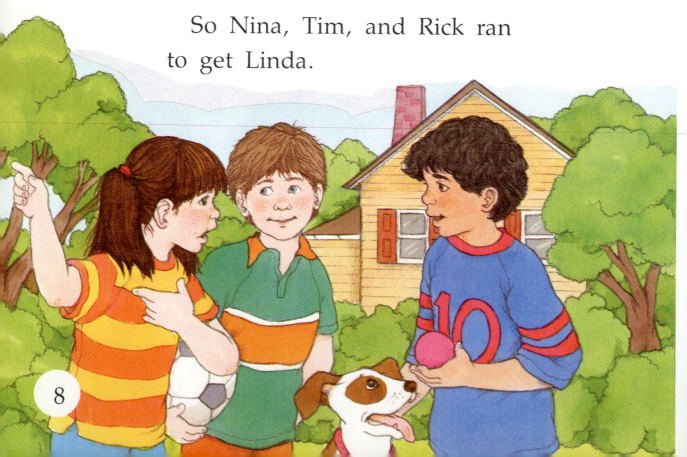

"Linda, follow us to see the
monster near Nina's house.
It is big and yellow," said Tim.

"It can dig up things," said Rick.

"It can push things, too," said Nina.

"Will it push me?" asked Linda.

"It will not push you," said Nina.
"You don't have to be afraid.
You will like to watch it."

So Nina, Tim, Rick, and Linda
ran to Nina's house.

"Here is the monster," said Nina.
"Don't go too near it."

"Oh, I know what that is,"
said Linda.

"This monster is big and yellow.
It's a helping monster," said Tim.

10

"It's big and yellow and helping.
But it is not a monster at all,"
said Rick.

Nina, Tim, Rick, and Linda see that the monster is just a bulldozer.
Now read to find out what a bulldozer can do.

The Bulldozer

by Edward D. Mullett

Look at this bulldozer.
It is big, and it is yellow.
A bulldozer can dig.
A bulldozer can push.
It can push many things.
It can push away very big rocks.

This bulldozer is pushing.
It is pushing away big rocks.
It is making a place for a new road.
It's making a place for a new school,
too.

This bulldozer is digging a hole.
It is digging a very big hole.
That hole is the place where the
new school will be.

Many girls will come down this
new road.

Many boys will, too.

They will go to the new school.

Pam and Jan both get new blue bikes.
How will Pam know her bike?
How will Jan know her bike?

Blue Bikes

by Margaret Braden

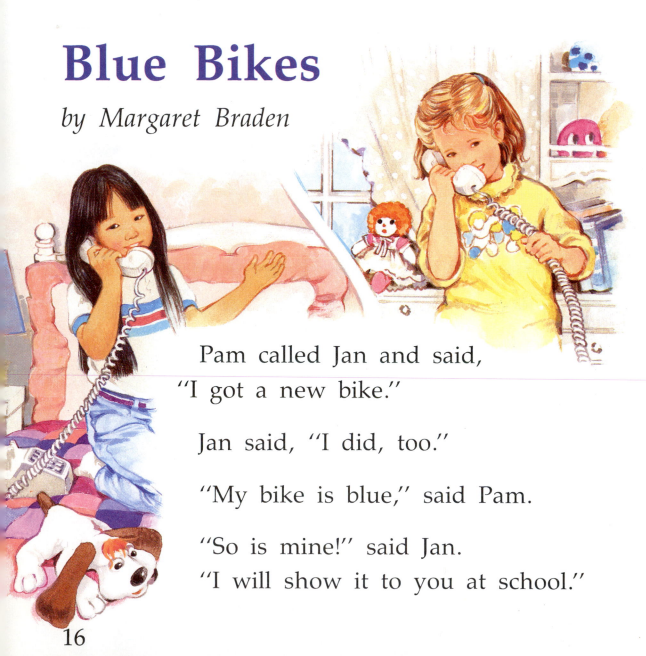

Pam called Jan and said,
"I got a new bike."

Jan said, "I did, too."

"My bike is blue," said Pam.

"So is mine!" said Jan.
"I will show it to you at school."

16

"You can see mine there, too," said Pam.

When Pam and Jan got to school, they looked at the bikes.

"Your bike is just like mine!" said Pam.

"Our bikes are just the same! I'm glad," said Jan.

Pam said, "So am I."

When the girls came out of school,
Pam asked Jan, "Is this my bike?"

"These bikes look just the same
to me," said Jan.

"I want to take my bike home,"
said Pam.

"I want to take my bike home, too.
Let's think what we can do,"
said Jan.

"My house is on this side
of the school.

So I came from this side.

I put my bike here," said Pam.

"My house is on that side
of the school.

So I came from that side.

I put my bike there," said Jan.

"This blue bike is mine,"
said Pam.

"Then this blue bike must be
mine!" said Jan.

At Pam's house her dad said,
"I got something for your new bike.
It is a tag with *Pam* on it.
I will help you put it on your bike."

"Oh, thank you, Dad.
I need this tag," said Pam.

Pam called Jan and said, "My dad got something for my new bike."

Jan said, "My dad got something for my new bike, too.
I will show it to you at school."

"I will show you what I got, too," said Pam.

At school the girls looked at the
tags on the bikes.

"My tag isn't like yours," said Jan.

"Our tags are not the same,"
said Pam.

"I'm glad our bikes are not just
the same now," said Jan.

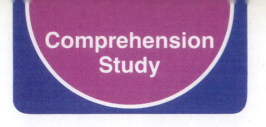

Sequence

Look at the pictures.
The pictures tell a story.
They show what comes first, next,
and last in this story.

A.

B.

C.

Why does picture **A** come first?
Why does picture **B** come next?
Why does picture **C** come last?

Now look at this picture story.

Which picture shows what comes first?
Which picture shows what comes next?
Which picture shows what comes last?

Now read these sentences from a story.

A. Nina comes to Pam's house.

B. Pam wants Nina to come to her house for lunch.

C. Nina and Pam have lunch.

Which sentence tells what comes first?
Which sentence tells what comes next?
Which sentence tells what comes last?

You have read some stories with colors in them. Now read to find out how you can mix colors to make a rainbow.

Paint a Rainbow

by Althea Rahz

Look at a rainbow.
What colors do you see?

Red, yellow, and blue paint
will help you make all the colors
of the rainbow.

Do this with the red paint.

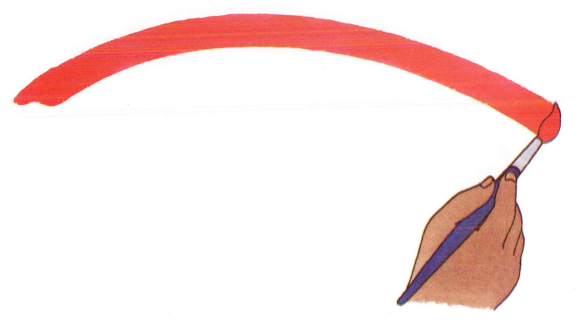

Now mix red and yellow paint.
What color did you make?
The color you made was orange.
Put orange next to the red.

The next color in a rainbow is yellow.

Put yellow next to the orange.

Now mix yellow and blue paint.

What color did you make?

The color you made was green.

Put green next to the yellow.

Put blue next to the green.

Now mix red and blue paint.
What color did you make?
Put purple next to the blue.

You have made a rainbow.
What colors do you see?

29

The Rainbow

There's a pot at the end of the rainbow,

That holds a treasure of gold.

There's a pot at the end of the rainbow,

With riches, so I am told.

—Anonymous

31

Thinking About "Rainbows"

In "Rainbows," you read about many people and many colors.

You read about Nina, her friends, and a yellow bulldozer.

You read about Pam and Jan and their new blue bikes.

You learned how to paint a rainbow, too.

As you read more in this book, look for stories that have colors in them.

1. What surprises did Nina in "The Yellow Monster" and Pam in "Blue Bikes" have for their friends?

2. Which colors from a rainbow did you find in these stories?

3. Do you think "Rainbows" is a good name for this unit? Why?

4. Which story did you like best? Why?

Near and Far

In "Near and Far," people will be looking for things that are near.

They will also be looking for things that are far away.

Will the people find what they are looking for?

If they find them, are these things near or far away?

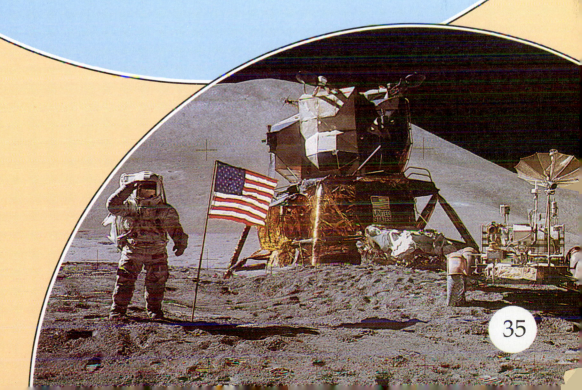

35

Read on Your Own

Sam Who Never Forgets by *Eve Rice*. *Greenwillow.* Elephant is sad because he thinks Sam forgot.

Pig Pig Rides by *David McPhail. Dutton.* Pig Pig rides his bike and pretends he's riding a motorcycle, a spaceship, and other things.

Goodnight, Horsey by *Frank Asch. Prentice.* A girl has a special horse ride before bedtime.

Tell Me Some More by *Crosby Bonsall. Harper.* Andrew tells Tim about a special place.

The Little Bird *by Dick Bruna. Price Stern Sloan.* A little bird looks for a place to build her nest.

Johnny Lion's Book *by Edith Hurd. Harper.* Johnny Lion's mom gives him a book when she finds out he can read.

Home Is Best *by Barbara Lucas. Macmillan.* Bitty Bear finds home is best when he tries to find out how far is far.

Fix-It *by David McPhail. Dutton.* By the time the Bears' TV gets fixed, Emma Bear is too busy reading to watch it.

Mr. Fig and his friends go looking for the sun. Where do they find it?

Mr. Fig Finds the Sun!

by Bernard Wiseman

Rabbit said, "I don't see the sun!
Is it lost?"

"No, it isn't lost," said Mr. Fig.
"There is a big cloud in the sky.
The cloud is over the sun.
So we can't see the sun from here."

"Look at those ducks," said Rabbit.
"Why are they flying away?"

"They are flying up to see the sun.
I want to see the sun, too.
I will fly with the ducks," said Owl.

"So do we, but we can't fly!
We don't have our magic hats
with us," said Mouse and Rabbit.

"I will take you up in the
Figmobile!" said Mr. Fig.
"We will follow those ducks!"

The Figmobile flew into the sky.
It flew up to the ducks.
Owl was with the ducks.

Owl said, "You flew up here
in the Figmobile!
Are you going to see the sun?
May I ride with you?"

"Yes, climb in!" said Mr. Fig.

"May we ride in the Figmobile
with you, too?" asked the ducks.

"Yes, climb in!" said Mr. Fig.

All the ducks climbed into the
Figmobile.
A big duck sat on Mr. Fig's hat.
The duck pushed the magic hat down.

41

"I can't see," cried Mr. Fig.
"I can't see where we are!"

Rabbit said, "A duck is sitting
on your hat, Mr. Fig."

"Get off, Duck.
Get off my hat!" cried Mr. Fig.

The duck got off Mr. Fig's hat
and sat down next to Mouse.

The Figmobile flew out of the clouds.
It flew over to some hills.

Mouse looked down at the hills.
"May we fly down and look at those trees on the hills?" asked Mouse.

Mr. Fig said, "I will land the
Figmobile on those hills."

They flew over the trees.
Mr. Fig landed the Figmobile.

"I see many yellow and red flowers over there," said Mouse.

"I see many orange trees over there," said Turtle.

"And I see the sun in the sky," said Rabbit.

"Now you can play in the sun!" said Mr. Fig.

45

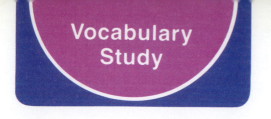
Antonyms

A.

B.

Look at these pictures.
Tell what these pictures show.

In picture **A,** where is the
Figmobile?

In picture **B,** where is the
Figmobile?

The words *up* and *down* are
opposites.

Now look at these pictures.
Tell what these pictures show.

In picture **C,** where do you see Owl?
In picture **D,** where do you see Owl?
In and *out* are opposites.

What do these pictures show?

In picture **E,** how does Mr. Fig feel?
In picture **F,** how does Mr. Fig feel?
Happy and *sad* are opposites.

Little Feet and Long Walk

by Florence Thompson

There was a boy.
His name was Little Feet.
Little Feet did not have a horse.

One day Little Feet asked his father,
"What must I do to get a horse?"

48

His father said, "You must find
a horse, my son."

So Little Feet went to look for
a horse.

"I hope I find a horse soon," said
Little Feet.

Little Feet walked a long, long way.
He did not find a horse.

Little Feet saw many hills.
He saw many trees.
He climbed up one hill.
He was tired.
So he sat down next to a tree
and went to sleep.

A horse climbed up the hill.
The horse saw Little Feet sleeping
next to a tree.

So the horse went to sleep, too.

When Little Feet sat up, he saw
the horse.

"I was looking for a horse.
Was this horse looking for a boy
like me?" he asked.

Little Feet walked up to the horse.
"Please be my friend," he said.
"Please come home with me."

Little Feet walked down the hill.
The horse followed him.
"I hope I can keep you," said
Little Feet.

Little Feet walked the long way home.
The horse followed him home.

"Father," Little Feet called.
"I have a horse.
Please may I keep this horse?"

"Where did you find the horse?"
his father asked.

Little Feet said, "I walked a long,
long way.
I climbed up a hill.
I was tired.
I went to sleep on that hill.
When I got up, I saw this horse.
I hope I can keep it.
It followed me all the way home."

Little Feet's father said, "You may keep this horse, my son.

You must give it food.

You must give it a name."

Little Feet said, "I will name the horse *Long Walk*.

I had to walk a long way to find this horse.

This horse had to walk a long way to find me."

A Wish Is Quite a Tiny Thing

by Annette Wynne

A wish is quite a tiny thing,
Just like a bird upon the wing,
It flies away all fancy free
And lights upon a house or tree;
It flies across the farthest air,
And builds a safe nest anywhere.

Eddie and his dad go to the zoo. Read to find out what Eddie tells his dad when they get home.

Eddie Couldn't Find the Elephants

by Edith Battles

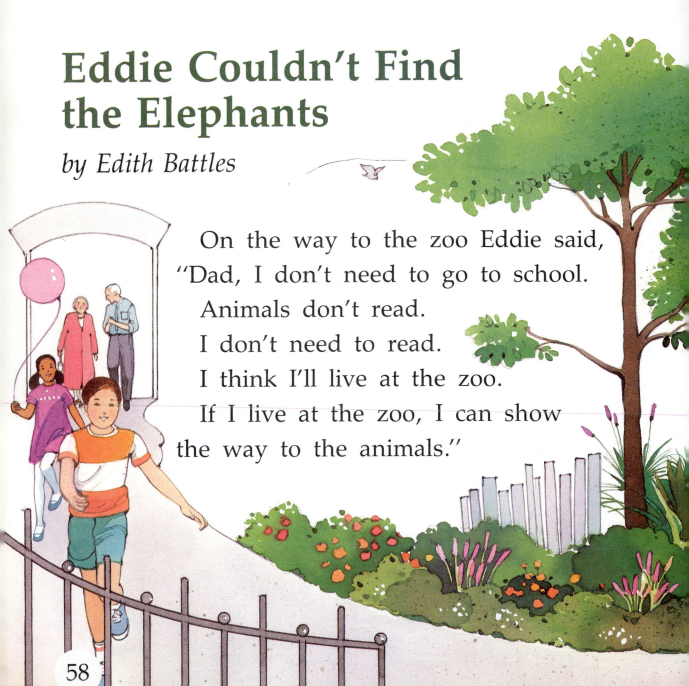

On the way to the zoo Eddie said,
"Dad, I don't need to go to school.
Animals don't read.
I don't need to read.
I think I'll live at the zoo.
If I live at the zoo, I can show
the way to the animals."

"Then show me the way to the animals," said Eddie's father.

"What animal will you show me first?"

"Elephants," said Eddie.

"Where are the elephants?" his father asked.

Eddie saw a sign that looked like it said *elephants*.

"This way," said Eddie.

ELEPHANTS

SEALS

The sign Eddie followed showed
the way to seals.

"Dad, let's look at the seals on the
way to the elephants," Eddie said.

Eddie and his father looked at
the seals.

Then Eddie saw a boy getting
some food.

"I want some of that," Eddie said.

When Eddie got the food, it was food for the seals.

It was not food for Eddie.
So Eddie fed the food to the seals.

"Dad, let's find the birds now," Eddie said.

Eddie looked up at the signs.

He waited for his father to read them.

Eddie's father waited for Eddie to read the signs.

ELEPHANTS

BIRDS

Then Eddie said, "Let's follow that sign."

So Eddie and his father followed the sign.

There were the elephants!
"I didn't want to find the birds," Eddie said.
"I just wanted to show you the elephants."

"Oh?" asked Eddie's father.

"Let's sit down and look at
these elephants," said Eddie.
"We can sit here.
I'll put this sign over here and . . ."

"Stop!" said his father.

But Eddie had sat in the wet paint.

WET
PAINT

"Go in there and see if the paint will come out," said Eddie's father.

Eddie saw the signs on the doors.
He looked at one sign.
He walked to that door.
Just then a girl came out the door.
Eddie ran over to the next door.

When Eddie came out, he did not say a thing to his father.

"Where do you want to go now?"
asked Eddie's father.

"Home," said Eddie.

At home Eddie said, "I don't think
I'll live at the zoo yet.
I think I'll go to school now.
I'll live at the zoo when I can read."

*Eddie saw elephants and
seals at the zoo.
Not all animals live at a zoo.
Read to find out where some
animals live.*

Animals

by Janet C. Bosma

You know that some animals
live in a zoo.

Animals that live in a zoo
may be from far, far away.

You could go to a zoo and
see these animals.

Some animals do not live in a zoo.

They live on a farm.

If you went to a farm, you could see these animals.

Some animals live here.
These animals do not want
you to see them.
Can you find the animal
in each picture?

Some of these animals could live
with you.
Each is a pet.
Do you have one of these animals?

Thinking About "Near and Far"

In "Near and Far," you read about people and some special things they were looking for.

Mr. Fig and his friends looked for the sun.

Little Feet looked for a horse.

Eddie looked for elephants at the zoo.

You read about some animals that were near to you and some that were far away.

As you read more stories in this book, look for other things that are near or far away.

1. How are Mr. Fig and Little Feet alike?

2. How are Mr. Fig, Little Feet, and Eddie different?

3. Is "Near and Far" a good name for this unit? Why?

4. Which story did you like best? Why?

Winks and Blinks

Do you know what a wink is?

A wink is one way of showing someone your feelings.

A wink can show a friend that you feel happy, or think something is funny.

It can also show that you have a secret.

Do you know what a blink is?

A blink is one way to show that you are surprised.

Being surprised is a feeling, too.

As you read the stories in "Winks and Blinks," look for ways people show their feelings.

What's Claude Doing? *by Dick Gackenbach. Houghton.* Claude's dog friends don't know why Claude won't come out to play.

Owl at Home *by Arnold Lobel. Harper.* Five stories about an owl who lives alone but is never lonely.

Feelings *by Aliki. Greenwillow.* Why do people feel happy, sad, or afraid? Read to find out.

Well, Why Didn't You Say So? *by Jo Wold. A. Whitman.* Why do we need words? This book tells you why.

Goodnight, Moon *by Margaret Wise Brown. Harper.* A bunny says goodnight to everything in the room before saying goodnight to the moon and going to sleep.

This Is the House Where Jack Lives *by Joan Heilbroner. Harper.* Jack takes his dog for a walk and has some surprises.

Whose Mouse Are You? *by Robert Kraus. Macmillan.* A little mouse saves his family and becomes very happy.

House of Leaves *by Kiyoshi Soya. Philomel Bks.* Sarah's new family makes a house of leaves into a home when it rains.

A girl wants to teach her dog to come, sit, and stay. How does the girl do this?

Charlie May Simon Book Award Author

Come! Sit! Stay!

by Joan M. Lexau

Tiny, you are getting big.
I will teach you some things.
I will teach you to come when
I say *come*.

I'll wait here.
Tiny, Tiny. Get over here.
Oh, I forgot.
I have to say *come*, or you
won't know what to do.
Come, Tiny. Come here!

That's great! You did it!
Tiny, you are a good dog.
Thank you for coming when
I called.
Let me hug you.

Let's do it again.
Tiny, come! Come to me.
That's a good dog.
How about a big hug?

Now let's play with this ball.

No, Tiny, don't jump on me!
Get off!
I don't like that.
We can't play with this ball.
I'll have to teach you to *sit*.
Then I can make you *sit* when you
want to jump on me.

Sit, Tiny, sit!
That's it. That's a good dog.

Let's see if you can sit again.
Sit, Tiny, sit!
No! No! No!
I didn't say to sit on me.

Get up, Tiny! Get up!

Oh, Tiny, I'm not mad at you.
You did sit.
That's a good dog.

Now I'll teach you to *stay*.
Stay!

Tiny, you are a good dog!
You stayed.
That's what I wanted.

No, don't get up yet.
Tiny, stay! Don't come.

Oh, no, I forgot!
You don't know about *don't*.
You came when I said *don't come*.
I have to hug you for coming, or
you will be all mixed up.

Let's see if you can do it all again.
Tiny, *Come!*
Tiny, *Sit! Stay!*

That's great! You did it all!
How about a big hug?
We will do this over and over
again.

Now let's go for a walk.

Oh, Tiny, I said a walk.
Go slow, Tiny!

Slow down! Slow down!
Stop, Tiny, stop!
Oh, help!

*Rosa and Paco want a little casa.
Read to find out what makes a big
or little casa special.*

The Little Casa

by Carolyn Wills

After school, Rosa and Paco go
to Mama and Papa's shop.
Then they all walk home.

One day, on the way home,
Rosa and Paco saw a playhouse
in Mrs. Long's toy store.

"Oh, Mama!" said Rosa. "Look
at that little *casa*!"

84

"It looks just like a big *casa*.
There is a place for a dog, too,"
said Paco.

"Oh, Papa," said Rosa, "may
Paco and I have this little *casa*?"

"Just now we need a new big
casa to live in," said Papa.

"The house we live in now is too
little for all of us," said Mama.

85

Mrs. Long's Toys

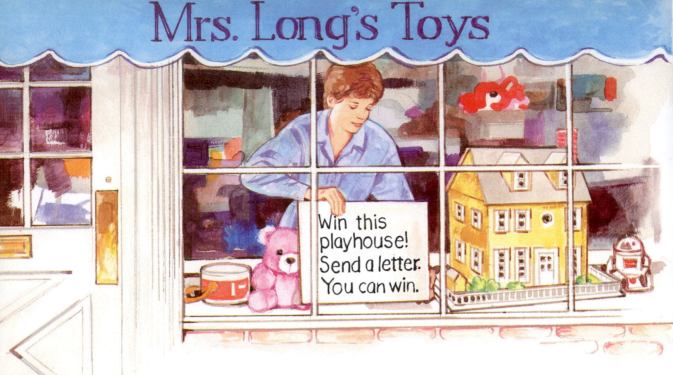

Win this playhouse! Send a letter. You can win.

Day after day, Paco and Rosa wished they could have the little playhouse.

Then one day there was a sign in Mrs. Long's toy store.
Rosa and Paco read the sign.

"We'll send a letter to Mrs. Long!" said Paco.

"I know our letter will win!" said Rosa.

This is Rosa and Paco's letter.

Dear Mrs. Long,
   Your little toy casa
looks just like the big
casa our Mama and Papa
want to have someday.
P.S. The little casa in
your shop needs something
special. Do you know what
that something special is?
We do.
Your friends,
   Paco and Rosa

Paco and Rosa waited and waited. Then one day, a letter came.

Dear Rosa and Paco,
I read your letter
and it was great!
Come to the store as
soon as you can.
Your friend,
Mrs. Long

The next day Rosa, Paco, Mama, and Papa went to Mrs. Long's toy store.

Mrs. Long asked, "What is the special something I forgot?"

Rosa looked at Paco.
Paco looked at Rosa.
Mama and Papa looked at them.

"You forgot people," said Paco.

Rosa said, "People are the most
special things in a little *casa,* or a
big *casa.*"

*What do the two owls in
this story wish for?
Who helps them? How?*

Two Hoots and the King

by Helen Cresswell

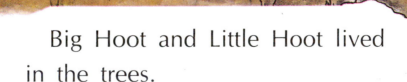

Big Hoot and Little Hoot lived
in the trees.

Big Hoot and Little Hoot were
not wise owls.

They were two very silly owls.

90

Wise owls went to sleep in
the day.

Big Hoot and Little Hoot flew
when it was day.

"I would like to be wise," said
Big Hoot.

"So would I," said Little Hoot.
"I don't like being so silly, but
I can't help it."

Just then Big Hoot saw something in a tree.

"Look over there!" Big Hoot said.

"What is that in the tree?"

"I see a yellow singing bird," said Little Hoot.

"It must be from the sun.

The sun is yellow, and so is this yellow singing bird."

"The sun is the king of the day," said Big Hoot.

"So the yellow bird must be the king of the sun!

Let's ask the king of the sun to give us a wish."

"What can we wish for?" asked Little Hoot.

"Let's ask the king of the sun
to make us wise," said Big Hoot.

"Oh, yes!" said Little Hoot.
"It would be good to be wise.
I would say wise things all day
and all night."

"Not all day," said Big Hoot.
"When you are a wise owl,
you will sleep in the day."

Big Hoot and Little Hoot flew
to the yellow singing bird.

"Good day, king of the sun,"
said Big Hoot.

"We know you are the king of the
sun," said Little Hoot.
"You are yellow like the sun.
We can see that.
We would like you to give us
a wish."

"What wish can I give you?" asked
the yellow singing bird.

"Can you help us to be wise owls?"
asked Big Hoot.

"I can make you a little wiser
than you are now," said the yellow
singing bird.

"Good, good," said the two owls.

"I am not the king of the sun,"
said the yellow singing bird.
"I am a canary!
Now you are wiser than you were!"

Then the canary flew away.

"We were very silly owls," said the two owls.

"Let's go to sleep."

And they did.

How Wise Is an Owl

by Ilo Orleans

He sits on the branch,
    And he blinks his eyes,
And people say
    He is very wise!

Never a smile—
    Just a frown or a scowl—
That's all I see
    When I look at an owl.

He's awake at night,
    He sleeps by day,
He thinks it is wise
    To live that way.

*Faces can show the way
people feel.
What are some of the feelings
that faces can show?*

What Faces Can Show

by Leona H. Biz

A face can show many things.
Look at this clown's face.
Does this clown look happy or sad?
How do you think he feels?

Did you say that the clown feels sad?

How do you think this clown feels?

People who see this clown's face
know that she is surprised.

How do you know that she is
surprised?

Look at this clown's face.

What can you tell about how this clown feels?

His face shows that he is happy.

Faces can show many things.

Faces can show you that people are sad.

They can show you that people are happy.

Faces can show you that people are surprised.

Faces can show you how people feel.

Follow Directions

Make a Clown Puppet

You just read about clowns. Now you can make a clown puppet. To make the puppet you will need:

Now follow the directions.

1. Glue two round plates to each other and to the

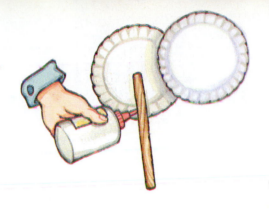

2. Cut out all the face parts you will need.

happy   sad

3. Once the face parts are made, make one side of the plate happy and one side sad.

4. Give your clowns a hat or a bow or something special.

Thinking About "Winks and Blinks"

In "Winks and Blinks," you read about some special feelings.

You read how Tiny surprised someone.

You saw how a little *casa* or house made people happy.

You read about a yellow canary who helped two owls.

You learned how faces can show how people feel.

As you read more stories in this book, look for feelings that people may have.

1. How were the little girl in "Come! Sit! Stay!" and Paco and Rosa in "The Little Casa" surprised?

2. Who were the helpers in the stories in this unit? How did they make people feel?

3. Is "Winks and Blinks" a good name for this unit? Why?

4. Which story did you like best? Why?

Old Days, Old Ways

In "Old Days, Old Ways," you will read some stories that happened a long time ago.

These stories are about the old days.

You will also read stories about things people did a long time ago.

These are the old ways.

As you read, look for the stories that tell about the old days.

Look, too, for the stories that tell about the old ways.

Read on Your Own

Coco Can't Wait! *by Taro Gomi. Morrow.* Coco goes to her grandma's house at the same time that grandma is on her way to Coco's house. Where will they meet?

Mr. Pine's Storybook *by Leonard Kessler. Grosset and Dunlap.* In this book you'll find more stories about Mr. Pine.

Harriet Reads Signs and More Signs *by Betsy and Guilio Maestro. Crown.* An elephant reads signs on a visit to town and finds Grandma's house.

It Looked Like Spilt Milk *by Charles G. Shaw. Harper.* This book shows you some cloud pictures you may have missed.

Small Plays For You and a Friend *by Sue Alexander. Houghton.* Do you like to put on plays with your friend? Now you can.

Aesop's Fables *by Michael Hague. Holt.* Here are some more stories from Aesop you will enjoy reading.

Mouse Tales *by Arnold Lobel. Harper.* In this book there are seven bedtime stories that Papa Mouse tells to his sons.

Harry and Jody want to get Grandma a special birthday surprise.

Why is the surprise they get Grandma a good one?

Grandma's Birthday Surprise

by Corrine C. Oldham

"Grandma's birthday is coming. What special present can we get for her?

What do you think she would like?" asked Harry.

"I don't know," said Jody. "Maybe Mother would know what Grandma likes."

"Mother, we need some help.
We can't think of a special present
for Grandma's birthday," said Harry.

"Your grandma likes things she
can use.
Will that help you think of
something?" asked Mother.

"We want to get Grandma a
special present," said Jody.

"If you made something for Grandma, that would be special," said Mother.

Harry said, "We could paint a picture for her."

Jody said, "Oh, no, Harry.
We can't give Grandma another picture.
That will not be special.
We paint pictures for her all the time."

114

"What is special that Grandma can use?" asked Harry.

Jody said, "Grandma likes to do things that are fun.
She likes to go for boat rides.
Another thing she likes to do is fish."

"I know what Grandma needs.
She needs a new fishing pole,"
said Harry.

Mother said, "I think you can get
Grandma a fishing pole.
She will like that.
It will be a great present."

That afternoon Mother, Jody, and
Harry went to get the fishing pole.
Harry and Jody walked over to
the little fishing poles.

Mother was looking at the big fishing poles.

She looked at Harry and Jody.

She saw the poles they had.

Mother said, "I know what will make this a special birthday for Grandma.

We'll get this big pole for her.

We'll get the little poles for you.

Then you and Grandma can have fun fishing."

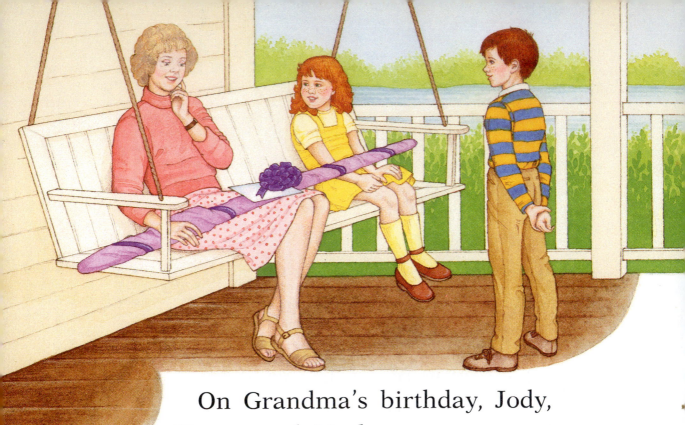

On Grandma's birthday, Jody,
Harry, and Mother went to
Grandma's home.

"Happy birthday," they all said.
"Happy birthday, Grandma!
We have a very special present
for you."

Grandma asked, "What can it be?"

Jody and Harry said, "Open it.
Open your present."

Grandma opened the present.
"This fishing pole is very special.
It is the one I have wanted for a
long time.
Thank you," she said.

Jody said, "We have another
surprise for you.
Mother got new fishing poles for
us, too."

Grandma said, "Let's all go
fishing this afternoon and try our
new poles.
This is a great birthday surprise!"

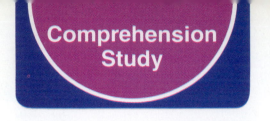
Relate Pictures to Text

Look at the picture.
Tell what it shows.

Read the sentences.

Which sentence tells about the picture?

How do you know?

1. Jody ran all the way home.
2. Jody painted a picture.
3. Jody went fishing.

Look at the picture.
Tell what it shows.

Now read the sentences.
Which sentence tells about the picture?
How do you know?

1. Grandma is climbing a hill.
2. Grandma is fishing with her fishing pole.
3. Grandma is opening her birthday present.

Signs help people in many ways. Now read to find out how signs can help you.

All About Signs

by Wanda Fortney

Signs tell us many things.
Some signs tell us things
with words.
If we can read, we can use signs
with words.

Some signs tell us things with pictures.

All people can use picture signs.

The pictures tell people what they need to know.

What do these signs tell us?

Look at these signs.
What do these signs say?
Where have you seen signs
like these?

Are there picture signs near your school?

Have you seen signs like these?

You may see picture signs near your home.

Have you seen signs like these?

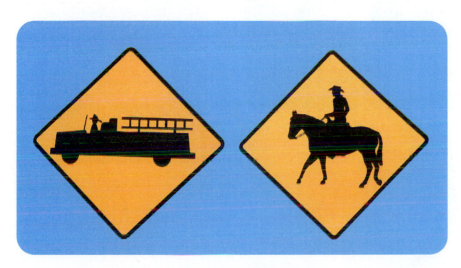

Have you seen picture signs
like these?

In what places could you see
these signs?

Tell what these signs say
to you.

Sometimes two signs
are used to make one
special sign.

Look at this sign.
What does it tell you?

Now look at this sign.
This sign is used to
say *no*.

Now what does the
sign tell you?

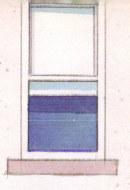

The Safety Song

by Margaret Lowery

We skip on our way to school
  each day,
We never like to be late;
Whenever we reach a traffic light,
We know the signal to wait.

The green light says "Go,"
  the red says "Stop";
A yellow light in between.
We look to the left and to the right,
And then we cross on the green.

Read to find out how Mr. Pine's signs help a little town.

Mr. Pine's Town

story and pictures by Leonard Kessler

Long, long ago there was a little town.

There were no signs in this town. The town did not have a name. People just called it Town.

The streets did not have names. So people had to say, "I live down that street."

One day a man came to the town
in a little red cart.

The people could not read, so
they asked the man,
"What's that on the side of
your cart?"

Pine's Signs

131

"That's a sign on my cart," the
man said.

"I'm a sign maker.

I will paint a sign for you.

What's the name of this street?"
the man asked.

"It does not have a name," the
people said.

"Well, it needs a name, and it needs a sign," the sign maker said.

"What do you want to call this street?" he asked.

"There are very big oak trees on this street," said a man.

"Let's call it Oak Street after
the oak trees," said a boy.

The sign maker painted the sign.
"See, this says *Oak Street*," he said
to the people in the town.
He put the sign on a pole.

"Oak Street!" they all shouted.

"I live on Oak Street," a girl said.

Day after day the sign maker made signs.

Soon all the streets in the town had names and signs.

The shops in the town all had signs.

Now all that was needed was a name for the town.

"What is your name?" the people asked the sign maker.

"My name is Pine," he said.

"Let's call our town Pineville after you!" the people shouted.

Mr. Pine painted a very big sign with the name *Pineville* on it.

Mr. Pine said, "Now I must go.
Your town has a name.
Your streets have names.
Your shops have names, too."

"Thank you, Mr. Pine, for all the signs," said the people of Pineville.

The people of Pineville could read now.

They could read all the signs.

137

Why does the boy in this play call "Wolf"?

What do the people of the town teach the boy?

The Boy Who Called Wolf

a fable from Aesop

These are the people who are needed for the play.

Narrator	**1st Person**
Boy	**2nd Person**
Sheep	**3rd Person**
Wolf	

Narrator: One day a boy sat on a hill.
He was looking after some sheep.
He needed to keep the wolf away from the sheep.
This boy did not like his work.

138

Boy: All day long, I look after the sheep.

All I see are sheep, sheep, sheep.

Sheep: Bah, bah, bah!

Day after day, all we see is this boy.

Boy: I don't see people.

I know what to do.

I'll play a trick.

I'll make people come to see me.

Narrator: So the boy played his trick.

Boy: Wolf, wolf! Help, help! The wolf is after the sheep! Help, help! Hurry, hurry!

Narrator: All of the people stopped working.
They ran up the hill to the boy.

1st Person: Where is the wolf? Tell us and we will get it.

Boy: There was no wolf.
I needed to see some people.
I played a trick to get you
to come up the hill.

2nd Person: It isn't nice to play tricks.

Narrator: The people turned and
went down the hill.
The boy looked down at them.
Soon the people were working.
Then the boy played his
trick again.

Boy: Wolf, wolf! Hurry, hurry!
Help, help! Hurry, hurry!

Sheep: Bah, bah, bah!
We see a boy.
We don't see a wolf.

Narrator: The people stopped
working and ran back up the hill.

3rd Person: Where is the wolf?
Tell us and we will get it.

1st Person: Do you need help?

Boy: No, I was just playing a trick.

2nd Person: It is not nice to play
tricks on us.
We have work to do!
You must not play this trick again.

Narrator: The people turned and went away.

They went back down the hill.

Just then, the boy saw a wolf!

The wolf was coming nearer and nearer.

The wolf was after the sheep.

Sheep: Bah, bah, bah!

Hurry! Get us some help!

Boy: Help, help! Hurry, hurry!

It's true. It's true.

There is a wolf now.

Please help me!

This is no trick!

Narrator: The people did not come.
They were down the hill.
They were working.
The wolf was getting nearer
and nearer.

Wolf: You have so many sheep.
They are so nice.
I think I'll take some.

Boy: Help me! Help me!
It's true! The wolf is here!
Help! Hurry! Please hurry!

1st Person: Let's go and see what that boy is doing.
Who knows? It may be true.
There may be a wolf.

Narrator: The people ran back up the hill again.
The wolf saw the people, turned, and ran away.

Boy: Oh, thank you, thank you.
Thank you for helping me.
I will not play a trick on
you again.
From now on, I will be happy
just to look after the sheep.

Narrator: The boy now knows it is
not nice to play tricks on people.
He will not play a trick again.

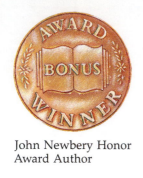

John Newbery Honor
Award Author

A little mouse and his mother go for a walk.
How does the little mouse feel about the clouds he sees in the sky? Why?

Clouds

story and pictures by Arnold Lobel

A little mouse went for a walk with his mother.

They went to the top of a hill and looked at the sky.

148

"Look!" said Mother.

"We can see pictures in the clouds."

The little mouse and his mother
saw many pictures in the clouds.

They saw a castle . . .

a rabbit . . .

a mouse.

"I am going to pick flowers,"
said Mother.

"I will stay here and watch the
clouds," said the little mouse.

The little mouse saw a big cloud
in the sky.
It grew bigger and bigger.

The cloud became a cat.

The cat came nearer and nearer
to the little mouse.

"Help!" shouted the little mouse,
and he ran to his mother.

"There is a big cat in the sky!"
cried the little mouse.
"I am afraid!"

Mother looked up at the sky.
"Do not be afraid," she said.
"See, the cat has turned back
into a cloud again."

The little mouse saw that this was
true, and he felt better.

He helped his mother pick flowers,
but he did not look up at the sky
for the rest of the afternoon.

Thinking About
"Old Days, Old Ways"

In "Old Days, Old Ways," you read stories that happened a long time ago.

You saw how a town was named.

You learned about a boy who almost tricked himself.

You also read about one way of showing someone that you love him or her.

Why do you think it's important to learn about the old days and old ways?

1. What special gifts were given in these two stories?

   "Grandma's Birthday Surprise"
   "Mr. Pine's Town"

2. Both the little mouse and the sheep were afraid of something. What frightened them? Why?

3. Is "Old Days, Old Ways" a good name for this unit? Why?

4. Which story did you like best? Why?

Word Helper

"Word Helper" develops readiness for dictionary skills and provides students with a reference for words they may wish to use in their writing. Example sentences for all new words in this book are provided. Illustrated sentences are followed by ■.

Aa

about I was **about** to read that sentence.

afraid I'm not **afraid** of a little frog. ■

after **After** lunch, we'll go out to play.

afternoon Let's go shopping this **afternoon.**

again Let's ride our bikes **again.**

ago He went out a long time **ago.**

animals   Those **animals** are mine. ∎

another   Here's **another** toy for you.

away   The rain will go **away** soon.

Bb

bah   All the sheep said, **"bah."**

became   The little boy **became** sad when his dog ran away.

better   I like this hat **better** than that one.

bigger   I need a **bigger** sign to tell the people where to run.

bikes   We'll ride our **bikes** home. ∎

birthday   It is Linda's **birthday.**

blue   Those flowers are **blue** and the others are red.

bulldozer   That's a yellow **bulldozer.** ■

Cc

came   Mother **came** home from work.

canary   Can the yellow **canary** fly? ■

cart   This big box will fit in that **cart.**

casa   **Casa** is another word for house.

castle   Long ago, a king lived in the big **castle.** ■

161

climb   Can you **climb** this tree?

cloud   Do you see the rain **cloud**?

clown's   A **clown's** tricks are silly. ■

colors   Flags come in many **colors**.

couldn't Paco looked but **couldn't** see the dog.

cried   "Look out, or you will fall!" **cried** Mother.

Dd

does   **Does** Pam know how to paint?

doors   The **doors** were painted red. ■

Ee

each

Each box had a purple name tag.

elephants

Elephants are big animals. ■

Ff

faces

Just look at all the happy **faces**! ■

far

Harry's grandpa lives very **far** away.

farm

Kim has cows on her **farm.** ■

father

Father worked on my bike.

felt

I **felt** good on my birthday.

first	Tiny is my very **first** pet dog.
flew	The plane **flew** above the clouds. ■
follow	We can **follow** this road.
forgot	I **forgot** my lunch.

Gg

glad	I am **glad** you like the toy I gave to you.
glue	I used **glue** to fix the toy. ■
green	The trees on Grandma's farm are **green.**
grew	The small frog **grew** bigger.

Hh

horse   I have a **horse** on my farm. ■

house   They live in a very nice blue **house**.

hurry   We must **hurry,** or we'll be last.

Ii

I'll   **I'll** take Jan to the toy store now.

if   I'll go home **if** you do, too. ■

Kk

know   I **know** how to mix paint. ■

Ll

land   The little plane will **land** soon.

last   Harry was the **last** one to get in line.

live   I **live** in the green house. ■

long   It's a **long** way to our boat.

lost   The boy **lost** his yellow balloon.

Mm

maker   My grandpa is a great cart **maker.** ■

making   Tim is **making** a toy boat.

166

many   The zoo has **many** animals. ■

maybe   **Maybe** we can go to the zoo.

mine   The nice blue hat is **mine.**

monster   Let's read about a **monster.**

most   **Most** people like surprises.

must   I **must** take my dog home. ■

Nn

name   Did you **name** your dog yet?

near   In school, Rick sits **near** Eddie.

nearer   Nina is **nearer** to the door.

next   Who plays with the ball **next**?

nice   What a **nice** present! ■

night   Can we see the sun at **night**?

Oo

off   Paco got **off** his bike.

once   **Once** Rick was home all day.

one   Harry has **one** bike. ■

open   I'll **open** the door for you.

or	Let's play ball **or** run.
orange	She has an **orange** balloon. ■
other	My **other** pet is a cat.
over	Rick came **over** to my house.

Pp

paint	I will **paint** the cart red.
parts	The toy cart has many **parts**.

people	**People** like to watch seals. ■
place	Here's a **place** to get food.

plate   Put this food on your **plate.**

please   **Please** help me with the cat.

present   My new dog was a **present.** ■

puppet   I can make my **puppet** do many things.

purple   Nina likes **purple** flowers.

push   Tim will **push** the cart.

Rr

rainbow   Did you see the **rainbow?** ■

read   I like to **read** about all the birds.

rest   I ran the **rest** of the way.

rocks   There are big **rocks** in the pond. ■

round   All the plates are **round.**

Ss

same   Those balloons are the **same.**

saw   I **saw** two ducks in the pond.

school   Girls and boys go to **school.** ■

seals	We saw the **seals** at the zoo.
seen	We have **seen** many rainbows.
sentences	The **sentences** tell a story.
sheep	The boy watched the **sheep.** ■
shouted	I **shouted,** "Stop!"
side	One **side** of the box is red.
sign	What's on the **sign**? ■
silly	That hat looks **silly.**
singing	Mama's **singing** is nice.
sky	The **sky** is a nice blue color.

sleep Grandma's dog will **sleep** here.

something Is **something** in my hand?

stay If I **stay,** will you play? ■

store Did you go to the **store**?

story Please tell us a **story,** Grandpa.

streets Ducks walked in the **streets**.

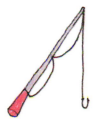

Tt

teach Will you **teach** me how to fish? ■

than   Do you think Pam is bigger **than** Jan?

those   I want to have **those** yellow hats.

tired   Playing made us very **tired.**

town   Our little **town** has only one school. ■

toy   For my birthday, I'll get one new **toy.**

trees   Those **trees** are very big. ■

true   This story is **true.**

turned   The cat **turned** and jumped.

two   **Two** dogs ran away.

Uu

use

Use two colors to make green. ■

Vv

very

We have a **very** nice school.

Ww

walked

Pam **walked** home for lunch.

was

It **was** fun to ride the bike.

watch

I like to **watch** the frog hop. ■

way   Let's go this **way** to school.

which   **Which** bird would you say is singing?

why   **Why** are the flowers blue? ◾

wiser   Friends can make us **wiser.**

wolf   There is a **wolf** in the zoo. ◾

won't   I know I **won't** fall off my bike!

words   My story has many new **words.**

work   Let's **work** in my dad's shop.

176

would   I think Tim **would** like to help.

Yy

yellow   He saw the **yellow** balloons. ■

Zz

zoo   We looked at the bears when we went to the **zoo.** ■

Word List

The following words are introduced in this book. Each is listed beside the number of the page on which it first appears. The words printed in color are words that students can decode independently.

The Yellow Monster
(6–11)

6 yellow
   monster
   ran
   house
   near
7 know
   if
   afraid
   watch
8 must
   dig
   follow
9 push

The Bulldozer
(12–15)

12 bulldozer
    many
    away
    very
    rocks
13 making
    place

road
school
14 hole

Blue Bikes
(16–23)

16 blues
    bikes
    got
    mine
    show
17 same
    glad
18 came
20 side
21 something
    tag

Sequence
(24–25)

24 tell
    story
    first

next
last
why
does
25 which
    read
    sentences

Paint a Rainbow
(26–29)

26 paint
    rainbow
    colors
27 mix
    was
    orange
28 green
29 purple

Mr. Fig Finds the Sun!
(38–45)

38 sun
    lost

cloud
sky
over
39 those
ducks
40 flew
into
climb
41 sat
42 cried
off
43 hills
trees
44 land

Antonyms
(46–47)

46 opposites
47 feel

Little Feet and Long Walk
(48–55)

48 long
walk
name
horse
one
father
49 hope

50 saw
tired
sleep
51 please
55 had

Eddie Couldn't Find the Elephants
(58–65)

58 couldn't
elephants
zoo
animals
I'll
live
59 sign
60 seals
61 fed
63 sit
64 doors

Animals
(66–69)

66 far
67 farm
68 each
69 pet

Come! Sit! Stay!
(76–83)

76 stay
teach
forgot
or
won't
77 coming
hug
again
about
ball
79 mad
83 slow

The Little Casa
(84–89)

84 casa
after
shop
playhouse
toy
store
86 wished
we'll
send
win
87 someday
88 as
89 people
most

Two Hoots and the King
(90–97)

90 two
   king
   lived
   wise
   silly
91 would
92 singing
94 night
96 wiser
   than
   canary

What Faces Can Show
(100–103)

100 faces
    clown's

Follow Directions
(104–105)

104 directions
    puppet
105 glue
    round
    plates

other
cut
parts
once
bow

Grandma's Birthday Surprise
(112–119)

112 birthday
    present
    maybe
113 use
114 another
    time
115 fish
116 pole
    afternoon
118 open

All About Signs
(122–127)

122 words
124 seen
127 sometimes

Mr. Pine's Town
(130–137)

130 town
    ago
    streets
131 man
    cart
132 maker
133 well
    oak
134 shouted

The Boy Who Called Wolf
(138–147)

138 wolf
    sheep
    work
139 bah
    trick
140 hurry
141 nice
    turned
142 back
144 nearer
    true

Clouds
(148–155)

148 top
149 castle
151 pick
152 grew
     bigger
153 became
       cat
155 felt
     better
     rest